Green Bay Packers Trivia Quiz Book

500 Questions on the Legends of Lambeau

Chris Bradshaw

ISBN: 1721926798
ISBN-13: 978-1721926794

Front cover image created by headfuzz by grimboid. Check out his great selection of sport, movie, music and TV posters online at:

https://www.etsy.com/shop/headfuzzbygrimboid

Introduction

Think you know about the Green Bay Packers? Put your knowledge to the test with this selection of quizzes on the legends of Lambeau.

The book covers the whole history of the franchise and includes the glorious Lombardi years, the Super Bowl resurgence under Mike Holmgren and Brett Favre and the modern-day successes of Aaron Rodgers and Mike McCarthy.

The biggest names in Packers history are present and correct so look out for questions on Favre, Rodgers, Reggie White, Donald Driver, Ahman Green, Jordy Nelson and many, many more.

There are 500 questions in all covering running backs and receivers, coaches and quarterbacks, pass rushers and punters and much else besides.

Each quiz contains a selection of 20 questions and is either a mixed bag of pot luck testers or is centered on a specific category such as the 1990s or defense.

There are easy, medium and hard questions offering something for Green Bay novices as well as professors of Packers history.

You'll find the answers to each quiz below the bottom of the following quiz. For example, the answers to Quiz 1: Quarterbacks, are underneath Quiz 2: Pot Luck. The only exception is Quiz 25: Anagrams. The answers to these can be found under the Quiz 1 questions.

All statistics relate to the regular season only unless otherwise stated and are accurate up to the start of the 2018 season.

We hope you enjoy the Green Bay Packers Trivia Quiz Book.

About the Author

Chris Bradshaw has written 20 quiz books including titles for Britain's biggest selling daily newspaper, The Sun, and The Times (of London). In addition to the NFL, he has written extensively on soccer, cricket, darts and poker.

He lives in Birmingham, England and has been following the NFL for over 30 years.

Acknowledgements

Many thanks to Ken and Veronica Bradshaw, Heidi Grant, Steph, James, Ben and Will Roe and Graham Nash.

CONTENTS

Quiz 1: Quarterbacks

1. Who is Green Bay's all-time leader in passing yards?

2. Who is the only Packers quarterback with a career passer rating of over 100?

3. Who holds the record for throwing the most interceptions in Packers history?

4. Which backup went 3-6 as a starter in 2017 after replacing the injured Aaron Rodgers?

5. Who holds the team record for the most passing yards in a single season?

6. Whose streak of 294 passing attempts without throwing a pick is the longest in team history?

7. Which Packer led the NFL in touchdown passes in 1983?

8. Who holds the record for the most touchdown passes in a single season?

9. How many TD passes did he throw to set that record?

10. True or false – Bart Starr never threw for over 3,000 yards in a single season?

11. Which quarterback holds the unwanted record of being sacked the most times in a single season?

12. Which backup quarterback threw for a franchise record 480 yards against the Lions on New Year's Day 2012?

13. Before Brett Favre, who was the last quarterback to start a playoff game for the Packers?

14. The Packers traded a first round draft pick to which team to acquire the services of Brett Favre?

15. Brett Favre and Aaron Rodgers are two of the four Packers quarterbacks to throw for over 4,000 yards in a season. Who are the other two?

16. Who holds the franchise record for the most 300-yard passing games in a single season?

17. True or false – Brett Favre threw 29 interceptions during the 2005 regular season?

18. Aaron Rodgers is one of two Green Bay quarterbacks to throw six touchdown passes in a single game. Who is the other?

19. Between the 2002 and 2004 seasons Brett Favre threw touchdown passes in how many straight games? a) 34 b) 35 c) 36

20. How many regular season touchdown passes did Brett Favre throw during his time with the Packers? a) 425 b) 435 c) 445

Quiz 25: Answers

1. Aaron Rodgers 2. Brett Favre 3. Vince Lombardi 4. Reggie White 5. Sterling Sharpe 6. Mason Crosby 7. Mike McCarthy 8. Ahman Green 9. James Lofton 10. Robert Brooks 11. Desmond Howard 12. Antonio Freeman 13. Josh Sitton 14. Dorsey Levens 15. LeRoy Butler 16. Don Hutson 17. Ray Nitschke 18. Clay Matthews 19. Randall Cobb 20. Davante Adams

Quiz 2: Pot Luck

1. Who holds the record for the most games played in team history?

2. What number jersey was worn by defensive superstar Reggie White?

3. Which head coach steered the Packers to victory in Super Bowl XXXI?

4. 'Golden Boy' was the nickname of which versatile Packer who was elected into the Hall of Fame in 1986?

5. Which head coach has the best winning percentage in team history?

6. Brett Favre threw his first touchdown pass as a Packer to which receiver?

7. What color is the facemask on the Packers helmet?

8. 'Mean On Sunday' was the title of which defensive star's 1973 autobiography?

9. Which Packers defensive lineman returned an interception for an 18-yard touchdown in the 2010 NFC Championship game against the Bears?

10. True or false – Up to the close of the 2017 season no Packers tight end had enjoyed a 1,000-yard receiving season?

11. In 2013, the Packers tied a franchise record after overturning a 23-point deficit to defeat which NFC team?

12. Who holds the record for being named NFC Offensive Player of the Week the most times in franchise history?

13. Who are the two players with 16 seasons of active service with the Packers?

14. In December 2005 the Packers routed which AFC South team by a score of 55-7?

15. Who was the Packers general manager from 1992 through to 2000?

16. Which former Packers offensive lineman was voted into the Pro Football Hall of Fame in 2018?

17. Which Packers defensive star required surgery after being hit in the face during a charity softball game in June 2018?

18. Whose amazing catch against the Vikings on Monday Night Football in November 2000 prompted commentator Al Michaels to famously say, 'He did what'?

19. What is the capacity of Lambeau Field? a) 81,441 b) 84,141 c) 88,114

20. What is the most points that the Packers have scored in a single regular season? a) 540 b) 550 c) 560

Quiz 1: Answers

1. Brett Favre 2. Aaron Rodgers 3. Brett Favre 4. Brett Hundley 5. Aaron Rodgers 6. Bart Starr 7. Lynn Dickey 8. Aaron Rodgers 9. 45 TDs 10. True 11. Aaron Rodgers 12. Matt Flynn 13. Lynn Dickey 14. Atlanta 15. Lynn Dickey and Don Majkowski 16. Aaron Rodgers 17. True 18. Matt Flynn 19. c) 36 20. c) 445

Quiz 3: Running Backs

1. With 8,322 yards who is Green Bay's all-time leading rusher?

2. Who rushed for 5,024 yards between 1971 and 1977?

3. Between 2010 and 2017 who was the only Packers back elected to the Pro Bowl?

4. Whose five rushing touchdowns between 1992 and 1997 are the most by a Packers back in playoff games?

5. Whose 1,435 rushing yards in 1997 are the third most by a Packers back in a single season?

6. In 1962, who became the first, and so far only, Packers back to lead the NFL in rushing?

7. Who fumbled twice in the first 69 seconds of the 2007 Divisional Round Playoff game but recovered to rush for a record 201 yards and three touchdowns?

8. Who holds the franchise record for the most rushing yards by a rookie running back?

9. Which back tied a franchise record after rushing for four touchdowns against Arizona in January 2000?

10. In 2003, Ahman Green rushed for a franchise record 218 yards against which AFC rival?

11. True or false – No Packers back rushed for more than 500 yards during the 2017 season?

12. Which back's 4,143 yards between 2007 and 2012 are good enough for fifth place on the team's all-time list?

13. Whose 671 career yards are the most by a Packers running back in playoff games?

14. Of Packers backs with over 750 rushing attempts, who has the highest average gain?

15. Which back set a franchise record after rushing for a touchdown in seven straight games in 1960?

16. Whose 81 rushing touchdowns between 1958 and 1966 are the most in team history?

17. You have to go back to 1990 to find the last running back picked by the Packers in the first round of the NFL Draft. Who was that back?

18. Who rushed for a rookie record 171 yards in a December 2005 game against the Lions?

19. How long is the longest rush in franchise history? a) 97 yards b) 98 yards c) 99 yards

20. Which backed rushed for that record long touchdown? a) Najeh Davenport b) Kenneth Davis c) Ahman Green

Quiz 2: Answers

1. Brett Favre 2. #92 3. Mike Holmgren 4. Paul Hornung 5. Vince Lombardi 6. Sterling Sharpe 7. Green 8. Ray Nitschke 9. B.J. Raji 10. True 11. Dallas 12. Aaron Rodgers 13. Brett Favre and Bart Starr 14. Tennessee 15. Ron Wolf 16. Jerry Kramer 17. Clay Matthews 18. Antonio Freeman 19. a) 81,441 20. c) 560

Quiz 4: Pot Luck

1. What number jersey did star quarterback Brett Favre wear?

2. Who were the first team to defeat the Packers in the Super Bowl?

3. Which safety is credited with creating the famous celebration known as the 'Lambeau Leap'?

4. Who was the first African-American head coach of the Packers?

5. What color jerseys did the Packers wear in Super Bowl I?

6. Before Clay Matthews in 2009 who was the last Packers rookie elected to the Pro Bowl?

7. Which Hall of Fame defensive lineman, who played for the Packers between 1960 and 1969, holds the franchise record for the most fumble recoveries with 21?

8. In 2012, which Packer became the first player in NFL history with over 900 receiving and 900 kickoff return yards in the same season?

9. In 2008, the Packers traded quarterback Brett Favre to which team?

10. What color is the Packers helmet?

11. True or false – Sterling Sharpe is the brother of former Denver Broncos tight end Shannon Sharpe?

12. Which long-time Packers executive entered the Pro Football Hall of Fame in 2015?

13. Brett Favre was born and raised in which state?

14. True or false – Between 2011 and 2017 the Packers were unbeaten in Thursday Night Football games?

15. The Packers pulled off an amazing come from behind victory over which team in December 2015 after Aaron Rodgers completed a 61-yard hail Mary as time expired?

16. Who caught that famous 61-yard reception?

17. Before becoming part of the NFC North the Packers were in which division?

18. Which former linebacker, who led the team in sacks in 1991 and 1992, has the same name as a famous crooner?

19. What was the name of the marching band that traditionally played at Packers games? a) The Lumberjack Band b) The Railroaders Band c) The Truckers Band

20. How many yards did Brett Favre throw for in his Packers career? a) 61,655 b) 65,561 c) 66,551

Quiz 3: Answers

1. Ahman Green 2. John Brockington 3. Eddie Lacy 4. Edgar Bennett 5. Dorsey Levens 6. Jim Taylor 7. Ryan Grant 8. Eddie Lacy 9. Dorsey Levens 10. Denver 11. False 12. Ryan Grant 13. Dorsey Levens 14. Gerry Ellis 15. Paul Hornung 16. Jim Taylor 17. Darrell Thompson 18. Samkon Gado 19. a) 98 yards 20. c) Ahman Green

Quiz 5: Receivers

1. With 743 career receptions who is Green Bay's all-time leader in catches?

2. With 1,519 yards, who holds the franchise record for the most receiving yards in a single season?

3. Brett Favre threw a record 99-yard touchdown pass against the Bears in 1995 to which receiver?

4. Who holds the record for the most 100-yard receiving games in franchise history with 32 between 1978 and 1986?

5. Who caught a touchdown pass in six straight games during the 2014 season?

6. Who is the only Packers receiver with over 10,000 receiving yards?

7. Up to 2018, just two Packers receivers had caught over 100 passes in a single regular season. Which two?

8. With 54 catches, who has more receptions in Packers playoff games than any other receiver?

9. Which Green Bay receiver caught 11 passes for 220 yards in a 1996 game against the 49ers?

10. In which round of the 1999 NFL Draft did the Packers select star receiver Donald Driver?

11. Brett Favre threw more touchdown passes to which receiver than any other?

12. Which receiver caught 13 passes against the Bears in October 2016, the second highest number caught by a Packer in a single game?

13. James Jones spent eight of his nine-year NFL career in Green Bay. He spent a single season with which AFC team?

14. The Packers last used a first-round draft pick on a wide receiver in 2002. Who did they select?

15. Who holds the team record for the most touchdown receptions in a single season?

16. How many touchdown passes did he catch to set that record?

17. Who caught a touchdown pass in five straight playoff games between 1997 and 2001?

18. Which Packer led the NFL in receptions in 1989, 1992 and 1993?

19. Who holds the record for the most touchdown receptions in team history? a) Donald Driver b) Don Hutson c) Sterling Sharpe

20. How many touchdown catches did he make to set that career record? a) 88 b) 99 c) 111

Quiz 4: Answers

1. #4 2. Denver 3. LeRoy Butler 4. Ray Rhodes 5. Green 6. James Lofton 7. Willie Davis 8. Randall Cobb 9. New York Jets 10. Yellow 11. True 12. Ron Wolf 13. Mississippi 14. True 15. Detroit 16. Richard Rodgers 17. NFC Central 18. Tony Bennett 19. a) The Lumberjack Band 20. a) 61,655

Quiz 6: Pot Luck

1. The name of the trophy awarded to the winning team at the Super Bowl is named after which Packers great?

2. Is the playing surface at Lambeau Field grass or artificial turf?

3. The Packers hold the NFL record for the most overtime games in a single season. How many sudden death games did they play in 1983?

4. Brett Favre made his debut for the Packers in 1992, in relief of which injured quarterback?

5. Which former Browns head coach was appointed the Packers defensive coordinator in January 2018?

6. In 2011, Aaron Rodgers became just the third quarterback in NFL history to throw three touchdown passes in a game 10 or more times in a single season. Who were the first two players to do so?

7. Excluding Curly Lambeau, who is the longest serving head coach in Packers history?

8. Which kicker appeared in 160 straight games between 2007 and 2016?

9. True or false – Between 1996 and 2006 the Packers won nine straight Sunday Night Football games?

10. In what decade did the famous 'G' first appear on the Packers helmet?

11. Which former running back was the team's offensive coordinator between 2015 and 2017?

12. True or false – In a 1965 game against Detroit Bart Starr was sacked 11 times?

13. Who caught his own blocked kick and ran it in for a 25-yard score to give the Pack an overtime win over the Bears in 1980?

14. What do the Packers have in common with the Redskins, Giants and Jets but not the other 28 NFL teams?

15. What is Brett Favre's middle name?

16. The largest attendance for a game involving the Packers was against which team?

17. The Packers have lost more playoff games in team history under which head coach than any other?

18. Do the Packers have a winning or losing record in games played on Thanksgiving Day?

19. What was the nickname of former defensive lineman B.J. Raji? a) The Freezer b) The Fridge c) The Hoover

20. What is the highest number of points the Packers have scored in a single game? a) 56 b) 57 c) 58

Quiz 5: Answers

1. Donald Driver 2. Jordy Nelson 3. Robert Brooks 4. James Lofton 5. Randall Cobb 6. Donald Driver 7. Sterling Sharpe and Robert Brooks 8. Jordy Nelson 9. Don Beebe 10. Seventh 11. Antonio Freeman 12. Davante Adams 13. Oakland 14. Javon Walker 15. Sterling Sharpe 16. 18 touchdowns 17. Antonio Freeman 18. Sterling Sharpe 19. b) Don Hutson 20. b) 99

Quiz 7: Defense

1. Who is Green Bay's all-time leader in sacks?

2. 'The Minister of Defense' was the nickname of which Packers great?

3. Which linebacker's 1,118 tackles are the most by a Packers player in team history?

4. Who holds the franchise record for the most interception return touchdowns with nine?

5. In 1989, who set the franchise record for the most sacks in a single season?

6. How many sacks did he record to create that record?

7. Which legendary linebacker's #66 jersey has been retired by the Packers?

8. Since 2000, who are the two Packers to have led the league in interceptions?

9. Which 1998 first-round draft pick holds the record for the most sacks in a single game after recording five against Buffalo in December 2002?

10. True or false – The Packers have never recorded a shutout in a playoff game?

11. In December 1980, the Packers gave up a franchise record 61 points to which divisional rival?

12. Which safety's 194 tackles in 2005 are the most by a Packer in a single season?

13. Who is the Packers' all-time leader in sacks in playoff games?

14. Which defensive back picked off 38 passes in a Packers career that ran from 1990 through to 2001?

15. Who are the three Packers to have recorded 10 or more sacks in at least four seasons?

16. Who returned an interception for a 99-yard touchdown against the Colts in October 2008?

17. Which much traveled linebacker and defensive end, who had two spells in Green Bay, is the only Packer to return three fumbles for a touchdown?

18. Which All-Pro defensive back tied a franchise record after picking off four passes in a 1978 game against San Diego?

19. What is the fewest number of points the Packers have given up in a single, 16-game regular season? a) 210 b) 215 c) 220

20. What is the most points that the Packers have given up in a single, 16-game regular season? a) 429 b) 439 c) 449

Quiz 6: Answers

1. Vince Lombardi 2. Grass 3. Five 4. Don Majkowski 5. Mike Pettine 6. Dan Marino and Tom Brady 7. Mike McCarthy 8. Mason Crosby 9. True 10. 1960s 11. Edgar Bennett 12. True 13. Chester Marcol 14. They have no mascot 15. Lorenzo 16. Dallas 17. Mike McCarthy 18. Losing 19. a) The Freezer 20. b) 57

Quiz 8: Pot Luck

1. Who is the only Packers defensive lineman to have had his jersey number retired?

2. Who are the two Packers to have caught 85 or more passes in three straight seasons?

3. Do the Packers have an overall winning or losing record in postseason games?

4. Who was Green Bay's head coach for 31 seasons between 1919 and 1949?

5. In what year did the Packers play their last home regular season game in Milwaukee?

6. What color jerseys did the Packers wear during Super Bowl XLV?

7. Who was the last non-kicker to lead the team in points scored in a single season?

8. Who led the team in sacks every year between 2009 and 2014?

9. What is the most games that the Packers have lost in a single season?

10. Which full back appeared in 188 games for the Packers between 1995 and 2006?

11. Do the Packers have a winning or losing record in overtime games?

12. The Packers signed star defensive lineman Reggie White after he left which team?

13. True or false – No Packer has led the NFL in single season sacks?

14. Since the AFL/NFL merger in 1970 who are the four Packers coaches to have steered the team to a division title?

15. Who was named the Packers general manager in 2005?

16. The Packers have their worst win percentage of just .286 against which AFC team?

17. In 2012, who set the franchise record for the most receptions by a Packers tight end in a single season after catching 61 passes?

18. The longest losing streak in team history stretched to how many games?

19. What is the fewest number of yards the Packers have gained in a single game? a) 36 b) 46 c) 56

20. How many interceptions did Brett Favre throw while with the Packers? a) 286 b) 296 c) 306

Quiz 7: Answers

1. Clay Matthews 2. Reggie White 3. A.J. Hawk 4. Charles Woodson 5. Tim Harris 6. 19.5 sacks 7. Ray Nitschke 8. Darren Sharper and Charles Woodson 9. Vonnie Holliday 10. False 11. Chicago 12. Nick Collins 13. Clay Matthews 14. LeRoy Butler 15. Reggie White, Clay Matthews and Kabeer Gbaja-Biamila 16. Aaron Rouse 17. Keith McKenzie 18. Willie Buchanon 19. a) 210 points 20. b) 439 points

Quiz 9: Special Teams

1. Who holds the record for the most successful field goals in franchise history?

2. Which Packer returned a kickoff 99 yards for a touchdown in Super Bowl XXXI?

3. Who was the punter on the Packers' 2010 World Championship-winning team?

4. Which defensive back scored three punt return touchdowns in his first two seasons with the Packers in 2013 and 2014?

5. Which receiver set a franchise record after returning a kickoff 108 yards for a score against the Saints in September 2011?

6. Which future Hall of Famer was the Packers kicker between 1980 and 1983?

7. True or false – No Packers punter has ever been voted to the Pro Bowl?

8. Who set a team record in 1993 after converting six field goals of 50 yards or more?

9. Who is the all-time leading point scorer in franchise history?

10. Which rookie's 95-yard touchdown against the Bears in 1974 remains the longest punt return in Packers history?

11. Which kicker converted 225 field goals during his time with the Packers between 1997 and 2005?

12. Which wide receiver returned a punt 76 yards for a touchdown in a December 2005 playoff game against the Falcons?

13. Which All-Pro kicker attempted a franchise record 48 field goals in 1972?

14. Which Packers offensive lineman, who played between 1958 and 1968, also kicked 29 field goals?

15. Who holds the record for the longest field goal in Packers history?

16. How long was that record-breaking kick?

17. Who holds the record for the most kick return touchdowns in franchise history after taking five to the house between 1967 and 1970?

18. Up to the start of the 2018 season, who was the only Packers kicker to have converted two field goals of 50 yards or more in the same game?

19. How long is the longest punt in team history? a) 70 yards b) 80 yards c) 90 yards

20. Mason Crosby holds the franchise record for the most successful field goals in a row after converting how many consecutive kicks? a) 21 b) 22 c) 23

Quiz 8: Answers

1. Reggie White 2. Sterling Sharpe and Jordy Nelson 3. Winning 4. Curly Lambeau 5. 1994 6. Green 7. Ahman Green 8. Clay Matthews 9. 12 games 10. William Henderson 11. Losing 12. Philadelphia 13. True 14. Dan Devine, Mike Holmgren, Mike Sherman and Mike McCarthy 15. Ted Thompson 16. Miami 17. Jermichael Finley 18. Nine games 19. a) 36 yards 20. b) 296

Quiz 10: Pot Luck

1. What color is the letter G on the Packers helmet?

2. What number jersey did quarterback Bart Starr wear?

3. In what year was Mike McCarthy appointed Green Bay's head coach?

4. How many World Championships did the Packers win in the pre-Super Bowl era?

5. Ahman Green set the franchise record for the most 100-yard rushing games in a single season in 2003. How many times did he break the century mark that year?

6. In what year did the Packers play their 1,000th regular season game?

7. Which Green Bay great was the subject of the award-winning biography 'When Pride Still Mattered'?

8. Up to the close of the 2017 season, which two teams had the Packers faced in the playoffs the most times?

9. Who recorded more wins while Packers head coach – Bart Starr or Mike Sherman?

10. Whose 190 games between 1958 and 1972 are the most in franchise history by a defensive player?

11. Kicker Mason Crosby wears what number jersey?

12. True or false – The Packers have never had the first overall pick in the NFL Draft?

13. Which Packer's pick six gave Green Bay an overtime win over the Seahawks in the 2003 Wild Card game?

14. Which quarterback, who has strong links with the Packers, threw that famous interception?

15. True or false – The capacity of Lambeau Field in its first season was just 32,500?

16. Which Packers receiver recorded a 1997 hip hop track called 'Down Wit' Tha Bay'?

17. The Packers have never lost a game at Lambeau Field against which AFC West team?

18. Which former Packers star won the 2012 edition of the TV talent show 'Dancing With The Stars'?

19. What was the name of the Packers center who went to seven straight Pro Bowls between 1957 and 1963? a) Jim George b) Jim Paul c) Jim Ringo

20. In 2015, the Packers wore throwback jerseys where the numbers appeared in a gold what? a) Circle b) Square c) Triangle

Quiz 9: Answers

1. Mason Crosby 2. Desmond Howard 3. Tim Masthay 4. Micah Hyde 5. Randall Cobb 6. Jan Stenerud 7. True 8. Chris Jacke 9. Mason Crosby 10. Steve Odom 11. Ryan Longwell 12. Antonio Freeman 13. Chester Marcol 14. Jerry Kramer 15. Mason Crosby 16. 58 yards 17. Travis Williams 18. Ryan Longwell 19. c) 90 yards 20. c) 23

Quiz 11: Aaron Rodgers

1. What number jersey does Rodgers famously wear?

2. In what year was Rodgers drafted?

3. With which pick did the Packers select Rodgers?

4. Rodgers' first NFL touchdown pass was caught by which receiver?

5. Rodgers played college ball for which team?

6. What is Rodgers' middle name?

7. Rodgers won his first regular season start against which division rival?

8. Who was the head coach during Rodgers' rookie season with the Packers?

9. In 2014, Rodgers threw 520 passes. How many of those were intercepted?

10. True or false – Rodgers appeared on a celebrity version of the TV quiz show 'Jeopardy'?

11. How many games did Rodgers start in his first three seasons in the NFL?

12. True or false – Rodgers is the only quarterback in NFL history to record a passer rating of over 100 in six straight seasons?

13. Who has caught more touchdown passes from Rodgers than any other Packers receiver?

14. Only one quarterback in NFL history has thrown for 200 touchdowns in fewer games than it took Rodgers. Which one?

15. Up to the close of the 2017 season Rodgers had been named the league MVP how many times?

16. Which two quarterbacks were taken in the first round in the same Draft that Rodgers was selected?

17. Rodgers is one of just four players in NFL history with 35,000 passing and 2,500 rushing yards. Who are the other three?

18. Rodgers was born and raised in which state?

19. Between 2008 and 2012 Rodgers threw touchdown passes in how many straight home regular season games? a) 34 b) 35 c) 36

20. In what year was Rodgers born? a) 1983 b) 1984 c) 1985

Quiz 10: Answers

1. White 2. #15 3. 2006 4. Nine 5. Ten times 6. 1996 7. Vince Lombardi 8. New York Giants and Dallas 9. Mike Sherman 10. Ray Nitschke 11. #2 12. False 13. Al Harris 14. Matt Hasselbeck 15. True 16. Robert Brooks 17. Denver 18. Donald Driver 19. c) Jim Ringo 20. a) Circle

Quiz 12: Pot Luck

1. Which team have the Packers beaten the most times throughout their history?

2. Who was the first Packer to make the Pro Bowl in each of his first four seasons in the league?

3. Who was the last Packers first-round draft pick whose full name starts and ends with the same letter?

4. Who are the two Packers head coaches with over 100 regular season victories?

5. Who returned an interception for a 70-yard touchdown in the Divisional round of the playoffs en route to Super Bowl XLV?

6. In November 2014, Aaron Rodgers threw six touchdown passes in a game against which NFC North rival?

7. Brett Favre is one of just two Packers to appear in over 200 regular season games. Who is the other?

8. Up to the close of the 2017 season the Packers had a losing playoff record against just two current NFL teams. Which two?

9. True or false – The Packers have never worn white jerseys in a home game at Lambeau Field?

10. In which round of the 2007 NFL Draft did the Packers select kicker Mason Crosby?

11. What number jersey does wide receiver Randall Cobb wear?

12. Which full back was a First-Team All Pro and Pro Bowl starter in 2004?

13. In a 1994 game against Miami Ed West became the first Packer to do what?

14. The Packers reached the playoffs for how many straight seasons before missing out in 2017?

15. Which head coach went 8-8 in his only season in charge in 1999?

16. True or false – Former Packers defensive coordinator Fritz Shurmur is the father of Giants head coach Pat Shurmur?

17. What do the initials A.J. stand for in the name of former linebacker A.J. Hawk?

18. Which college has produced the most Packers in team history?

19. What was the nickname of former Packers linebacker Tony Bennett? a) Alligator b) Crocodile c) Dinosaur

20. By what name was Hall of Fame runner and receiver John McNally better known? a) Johnny Blood b) Johnny Guts c) Johnny Thunder

Quiz 11: Answers

1. #12 2. 2005 3. 24th 4. Greg Jennings 5. California Golden Bears 6. Charles 7. Minnesota 8. Mike Sherman 9. Five 10. True 11. None 12. True 13. Jordy Nelson 14. Dan Marino 15. Twice 16. Alex Smith and Jason Campbell 17. Fran Tarkenton, Donovan McNabb and John Elway 18. California 19. b) 35 games 20. a) 1983

Quiz 13: 1960s / 1970s

1. Which team did the Packers defeat in Super Bowl I?

2. What was the final score in Super Bowl I?

3. Who was named the game's Most Valuable Player?

4. Super Bowl I was hosted at which famous stadium?

5. Which team did the Packers defeat in Super Bowl II?

6. What was the final score in that second Super Bowl triumph?

7. What venue hosted Super Bowl II?

8. Who won the MVP award at Super Bowl II?

9. Which head coach steered the Packers to their first two Super Bowl triumphs?

10. Who was the Packers head coach from 1968 through to 1970?

11. The Packers won back-to-back NFL Championships in 1961 and 1962 defeating which team in the title game both times?

12. The Packers were the last team to win the NFL Championship in the pre-Super Bowl era. Which team did they beat to become 1965 champions?

13. Which alliteratively-named head coach was in charge of the Packers between 1971 and 1974?

14. True or false – No Packers quarterback was elected to the Pro Bowl in the 1970s?

15. Which former player was named the team's head coach in 1975?

16. The Packers reached both Super Bowls I and II after defeating which team in the NFL Championship Game?

17. Which offensive star did the Packers select with the sixth pick of the 1978 NFL Draft?

18. The Packers were beaten just once in the NFL Championship game in the 1960s. Which team defeated them to claim the 1960 crown?

19. What was the fewest number of games won by the Packers during a single season during the 1960s and 1970s? a) Three b) Four c) Five

20. How many times did the Packers reach the playoffs during the 1970s? a) Once b) Twice c) Three times

Quiz 12: Answers

1. Detroit 2. Clay Matthews 3. Kenny Clark 4. Curly Lambeau and Mike McCarthy 5. Tramon Williams 6. Chicago 7. Donald Driver 8. Denver and Philadelphia 9. False 10. Sixth 11. #18 12. William Henderson 13. Catch a two-point conversion 14. Eight 15. Ray Rhodes 16. False 17. Aaron James 18. Notre Dame 19. a) Alligator 20. a) Johnny Blood

Quiz 14: Pot Luck

1. Which Minnesota quarterback threw a record six touchdown passes in a 1986 game against the Packers?

2. Who won more games while head coach of the Packers – Forrest Gregg or Lindy Infante?

3. Which defensive back did the Packers select with their first pick in the 2018 NFL Draft?

4. What jersey number did running back John Kuhn wear?

5. Who scored four touchdowns and converted six extra points and a field goal for a team record 33 points in a 1961 game against the Colts?

6. Which alliteratively-named receiver came off the bench to catch seven passes for 138 yards and two touchdowns in Super Bowl I?

7. Who caught Brett Favre's first NFL completion?

8. What color jerseys did the Packers wear in Super Bowl XXXII?

9. In 1999, whom did the Green Bay Press Gazette crown as the Packers Player of the Century?

10. True or false – The Packers have provided more players to the Pro Football Hall of Fame than any other franchise?

11. The longest post-season streak in franchise history saw the Packers reach the playoffs in how many straight seasons?

12. Curly Lambeau is the only person in Packers history to wear what number jersey?

13. 'The Ginger Wolverine' was the nickname of which former Packers punter?

14. Which former Packers kicker has won the American Century Championship celebrity golf tournament?

15. Which Hall of Famer's #14 jersey has been retired by the Packers?

16. Which Super Bowl-winning player with Washington became the Packers President and CEO in 2008?

17. Whose 113 tackles in 2006 were the most in a season by a defensive lineman in franchise history?

18. The longest winning run in franchise history stretched to how many games between 2010 and 2011?

19. Which college has provided the Packers with the most first-round draft picks? a) Alabama b) Notre Dame c) Minnesota

20. What is the most net yards that the Packers have gained in a single season? a) 6,282 b) 6,382 c) 6,482

Quiz 13: Answers

1. Kansas City 2. Packers 35-10 Chiefs 3. Bart Starr 4. Los Angeles Memorial Coliseum 5. Oakland 6. Packers 33-14 Raiders 7. Orange Bowl 8. Bart Starr 9. Vince Lombardi 10. Phil Bengtson 11. New York Giants 12. Cleveland 13. Dan Devine 14. True 15. Bart Starr 16. Dallas 17. James Lofton 18. Philadelphia Eagles 19. b) Four 20. a) Once

Quiz 15: 1980s

1. Who was the Packers head coach at the start of the 1980s?

2. Which California quarterback did the Packers select with the sixth overall pick of the 1981 NFL Draft?

3. In September 1982, the Packers turned a 0-23 deficit into a 35-23 victory over which team?

4. The 1982 Packers were one and done in the playoffs, losing to which team?

5. In October 1983, the Packers were on the right side of a crazy 48-47 score against which NFC East team?

6. The Packers had back-to-back 8-8 seasons in 1984 and 1985 under which head coach?

7. How many division titles did the Packers win throughout the 1980s?

8. True or false – No Packer rushed for over 1,000 yards in a season during the 1980s?

9. Who were the two quarterbacks to throw 25 or more touchdown passes in a season during the 1980s?

10. Three Packers led the team in receptions in a season in the 1980s. Which three?

11. Which pass rusher led the team in sacks in 1986, 1987, 1988 and 1989?

12. Del Rodgers was the only Packer to do what throughout the whole of the 1980s?

13. In which round of the 1988 NFL Draft did the Packers select Sterling Sharpe?

14. Which defensive back, who entered the Packers Hall of Fame in 2017, intercepted nine passes in 1986?

15. Who was the only Packers quarterback elected to the Pro Bowl during the 1980s?

16. Bucky Scribner, Joe Prokop and Don Bracken all played which position for the Packers during the 1980s?

17. In 1988, which linebacker became the first, and so far only, Packers player to record two safeties in the same season?

18. Which receiver's 13 touchdowns in 1989 were the most by a Packer in a single season during the 1980s?

19. What was the most wins recorded by the Packers in a single season in the 1980s? a) Eight b) Nine c) Ten

20. What was the lowest number of wins recorded by the packers during a single season during the 1980s? a) Three b) Four c) Five

Quiz 14: Answers

1. Tommy Kramer 2. Forrest Gregg 3. Jaire Alexander 4. #30 5. Paul Hornung 6. Max McGee 7. Brett Favre (from a deflection) 8. White 9. Don Hutson 10. False – They're second behind the Bears 11. Eight 12. #1 13. Tim Masthay 14. Al Del Greco 15. Don Hutson 16. Mark Murphy 17. Aaron Kampman 18. 15 games 19. c) Minnesota 20. c) 6,482 yards

Quiz 16: Pot Luck

1. What is the name of Green Bay's fight song?

2. Which legendary Packer appeared alongside The Monkees in the 1968 movie 'Head'?

3. What is the highest number of games the Packers have won in a single regular season?

4. Which full back was a 2014 First-Team All Pro and Pro Bowl starter?

5. In January 1983, the Packers won their first playoff game in 15 years, defeating which team 41-16 in the Wild Card game?

6. What was long-time coach Curly Lambeau's real first name?

7. Which Packers great appears on Twitter using the handle @Leap36?

8. The Packers have endured more defeats against which team than any other?

9. What do the Packers have in common with the Bears, Bills, Browns, Giants and Steelers?

10. KGB was the nickname of which former Packers defensive star?

11. In what year did Lambeau Field open?

12. Before Jaire Alexander in 2018, who was the last player chosen by the Packers in the first round of the NFL Draft whose surname started with a vowel?

13. True or false – The Packers didn't appear on Monday Night Football for six straight seasons in the late 1980s and early 1990s?

14. Which former Packers great wrote a series of children's books called 'Quickie Handles a Loss', 'Quickie Makes the Team', and 'Quickie Goes to the Big Game'?

15. Who are the five Green Bay head coaches with an overall winning record with the Packers?

16. The half-time show at Super Bowl XXXI was based on music from which cult classic movie?

17. Between 1968 and 1991 the Packers had how many winning seasons?

18. In what year did Green Bay City Stadium officially become known as Lambeau Field?

19. Who holds the franchise record for scoring the most touchdowns in a single season? a) Ahman Green b) Don Hutson c) Sterling Sharpe

20. How many touchdowns did he score to set that record? a) 18 b) 19 c) 20

Quiz 15: Answers

1. Bart Starr 2. Rich Campbell 3. L.A. Rams 4. Dallas 5. Washington 6. Forrest Gregg 7. One 8. True 9. Lynn Dickey and Don Majkowski 10. James Lofton, Walter Stanley and Sterling Sharpe 11. Tim Harris 12. Return a kickoff for a TD 13. First 14. Mark Lee 15. Don Majkowski 16. Punter 17. Tim Harris 18. Sterling Sharpe 19. c) Ten 20. b) Four

Quiz 17: 1996 World Champions

1. The 1996 Packers became World Champions after defeating which team in Super Bowl XXXI?

2. What was the score in that game?

3. Which stadium hosted Super Bowl XXXI?

4. Who was named the MVP of Super Bowl XXXI?

5. Brett Favre threw an 81-yard touchdown pass to which receiver during the second quarter of Super Bowl XXXI?

6. Which R&B singer performed the national anthem at Super Bowl XXXI?

7. Who was the only Packer to score a rushing touchdown in Super Bowl XXXI?

8. Which Packer recorded three sacks during Super Bowl XXXI?

9. The Packers defense intercepted which quarterback four times during Super Bowl XXXI?

10. True or false – The Packers were the first team wearing colored jerseys to win a Super Bowl hosted indoors?

11. Which team did the 1996 Packers defeat in the Divisional Round Playoff?

12. The Packers reached Super Bowl XXXI after beating which team in the NFC Championship game?

13. Who was the defensive coordinator on the Super Bowl XXXI-winning team?

14. Who was the offensive coordinator on the 1996 World Championship team?

15. Which Green Bay tight end caught a two-point conversion during Super Bowl XXXI?

16. Who was the referee in Super Bowl XXXI?

17. Who was the backup quarterback on the 1996 World Championship-winning team?

18. Which current NFL head coach was the Packers tight ends coach during the 1996 World Championship season?

19. How many games did the Packers win during the 1996 regular season? a) 12 b) 13 c) 14

20. Who was the leading rusher on the 1996 World Champion team? a) Edgar Bennett b) William Henderson c) Dorsey Levens

Quiz 16: Answers

1. Go! You Packers! Go! 2. Ray Nitschke 3. 15 games 4. John Kuhn 5. St Louis Cardinals 6. Earl 7. LeRoy Butler 8. Chicago Bears 9. They don't have cheerleaders 10. Kabeer Gbaja-Biamila 11. 1957 12. Antuan Edwards in 1999 13. True 14. Donald Driver 15. Vince Lombardi, Curly Lambeau, Mike McCarthy, Mike Sherman and Mike Holmgren 16. The Blues Brothers 17. Four 18. 1965 19. a) Ahman Green 20. c) 20

Quiz 18: 1990s

1. Who was Green Bay's head coach at the start of the 1990s?

2. The Packers had the same regular season win loss record in each of Mike Holmgren's first three seasons with the Packers. What was it?

3. Which team eliminated the 1993, 1994 and 1995 Packers from the playoffs?

4. Which former Chicago Bears quarterback led the team in passing in 1991, throwing for 1,490 yards and 11 touchdowns?

5. The Packers reached Super Bowl XXXII after defeating which team in the NFC Championship game?

6. Brett Favre threw his first game-winning touchdown pass as a Packer to which receiver against the Bengals in September 1992?

7. Which Packers defensive back was named a First-Team All-Pro in 1993, 1996, 1997 and 1998?

8. Which Packers kicker was voted to the Pro Bowl for the first and only time in 1993?

9. The 1993 Packers won their first playoff game in 11 years, scoring a last-minute touchdown to defeat which rival 28-24?

10. Who caught the 40-yard touchdown pass that gave the Packers that famous win?

11. How many division titles did the Packers win during the 1990s?

12. What was the fewest number of wins recorded by the Packers in a regular season with Mike Holmgren as head coach?

13. Who succeeded Mike Holmgren as the Packers head coach?

14. In 1997, which running back became the first Packer to make the Pro Bowl roster as a special-teams cover specialist?

15. Who were the two Packers tight ends with over 50 receptions in a single season during the 1990s?

16. True or false – In 1998, the Packers' leading rusher amassed just 386 yards?

17. Mike Holmgren's last game as Packers head coach was a 30-27 Wild Card loss to which team?

18. How many losing seasons did the Packers record during the whole of the 1990s?

19. The 1996 World Champion Packers led the league in scoring. How many points did they amass during the regular season? a) 446 b) 456 c) 466

20. In the same season, the Packers also had the NFL's stingiest defense. How many points did they give up? a) 226 b) 236 c) 246

Quiz 17: Answers

1. New England 2. Packers 35-21 Patriots 3. Louisiana Superdome 4. Desmond Howard 5. Antonio Freeman 6. Luther Vandross 7. Brett Favre 8. Reggie White 9. Drew Bledsoe 10. True 11. San Francisco 12. Carolina 13. Fritz Shurmur 14. Sherman Lewis 15. Mark Chmura 16. Gerald Austin 17. Jim McMahon 18. Andy Reid 19. b) 13 games 20. a) Edgar Bennett

Quiz 19: 2000s

1. Who was the Packers head coach at the start of the 2000 season?

2. Which future Pro Bowl tight end did the Packers select with their first pick in the 2000 NFL Draft?

3. How many games did the Packers win during Mike McCarthy's first season as head coach?

4. Two Packers had over 1,000 receiving yards in 2004. Which two?

5. In the early 2000s, who became the first Packer to record 10 or more sacks in three successive seasons?

6. Who led the team in interceptions for five straight years between 2000 and 2004?

7. Which two defensive stars did the Packers select in the first round of the 2009 NFL Draft?

8. The 2007 Packers famously defeated which team 42-20 in a snowy Divisional Round playoff?

9. The Packers sent a sixth-round draft pick in 2007 to which team to secure the services of running back Ryan Grant?

10. The 2007 Packers were eliminated from the playoffs in the NFC Championship game, losing 23-20 to which team?

11. In October 2005, the Packers thrashed which NFC South team 52-3?

12. In December 2005, the Packers were routed by a score of 45-3 by which AFC North team?

13. Brett Favre threw his final touchdown pass in Packers colors in the 2007 NFC Championship Game to which receiver?

14. What was the most regular season games won by the Packers during a single season in the 2000s?

15. What was the lowest number of wins recorded in a single season by the Packers during the 2000s?

16. Between 2000 and 2009 the Packers won how many division titles?

17. Who were the two Packers backs to rush for over 1,000 yards in a season during the 2000s?

18. Did the Packers have an overall winning or losing record throughout the whole of the 2000s?

19. How many losing seasons did the Packers record during the 2000s? a) One b) Two c) Three

20. In 2003, the Packers set a franchise record for rushing yards. How many did they gain? a) 2,338 b) 2,448 c) 2,558

Quiz 18: Answers

1. Lindy Infante 2. 9-7 3. Dallas 4. Mike Tomczak 5. San Francisco 6. Kitrick Taylor 7. LeRoy Butler 8. Chris Jacke 9. Detroit 10. Sterling Sharpe 11. Three 12. Nine wins 13. Ray Rhodes 14. Travis Jervey 15. Mark Chmura and Jackie Harris 16. True 17. San Francisco 18. Two 19. b) 456 20. c) 246

Quiz 20: Pot Luck

1. Who spent more seasons as head coach of the Packers – Vince Lombardi or Mike Holmgren?

2. In January 2003, who became the first team to defeat the Packers in a playoff game at Lambeau Field?

3. Throughout the history of the franchise do the Packers have a winning or losing record in road games?

4. Who are the two Packers head coaches to record 21 regular season wins in their first two seasons in charge?

5. Who is the play-by-play announcer on Packers radio commentaries?

6. Which long-serving center is the color commentator on Packers radio broadcasts?

7. True or false – The Packers appeared on Monday Night Football five times in 2005 and 2006 and lost every time?

8. In October 2012, Aaron Rodgers threw a team-record six touchdown passes against which AFC South team?

9. Who holds the record for the most Pro Bowl appearances by a Packers receiver with seven?

10. Which Green Bay great was the author of the best-selling book 'Instant Replay'?

11. In December 2015, the Packers came back from a 0-20 scoreline to defeat which division rival 27-23?

12. True or false – The US Navy has a warship called USS Green Bay?

13. Which two-time Super Bowl-winning head coach was the receivers coach in Green Bay in 1986 and 1987?

14. Which Viking tied an NFL record after returning a kickoff 109 yards for a touchdown against the Packers in October 2013?

15. Lambeau Field is the longest continuously occupied stadium in the NFL. Opening in 1972, which venue is the second on that list?

16. Whom did Mike Holmgren succeed as Green Bay head coach?

17. Which former Packers offensive lineman was the author of a book called, 'My Dirty Little Secrets—Steroids, Alcohol & God'?

18. Who returned a pick 95 yards for a touchdown against the Saints in October 2005?

19. What is the warmest temperature recorded at a Packers home game? a) 75F b) 85F c) 95F

20. Since their foundation up to 2018 the Packers have had how many head coaches? a) 14 b) 16 c) 18

Quiz 19: Answers

1. Mike Sherman 2. Bubba Franks 3. Eight 4. Javon Walker and Donald Driver 5. Kabeer Gbaja-Biamila 6. Darren Sharper 7. B.J. Raji and Clay Matthews 8. Seattle 9. New York Giants 10. New York Giants 11. New Orleans 12. Baltimore 13. Donald Lee 14. 13 games 15. Four wins 16. Four 17. Ahman Green and Ryan Grant 18. Winning 19. b) Two 20. c) 2,558

Quiz 21: 2010 World Champions

1. Which team did the Packers face in Super Bowl XLV?

2. What was the final score in the big game?

3. Which venue hosted Super Bowl XLV?

4. Who was named the game's Most Valuable Player?

5. Who opened the scoring with a 29-yard touchdown catch?

6. Which wide receiver caught 21 and 8-yard touchdown passes in the second and fourth quarters?

7. Which Packers defender scored a 37-yard interception return touchdown?

8. Four Packers offensive starters in Super Bowl XLV had first names and surnames that started with the same letter. Name the quartet.

9. The 2010 Packers entered the playoffs as what number seed in the NFC?

10. Aaron Rodgers started 15 of 16 regular season games in 2010. Who started in the game that Rodgers missed?

11. Which team did the Packers defeat in the Wild Card game?

12. The Packers routed which team 48-21 in the Divisional Round?

13. The Packers reached Super Bowl XLV after beating which team in the NFC Championship game?

14. Who led the team in sacks in 2010 with 13.5?

15. The Packers finished the 2010 regular season with how many wins?

16. Which versatile Hall of Famer performed the coin toss at Super Bowl XLV?

17. Who sang the National Anthem at Super Bowl XLV?

18. Which band headlined the half-time show at Super Bowl XLV?

19. Who led the team in rushing yards during the 2010 regular season? a) Brandon Jackson b) John Kuhn c) Aaron Rodgers

20. The Packers defense ranked second in the NFL in 2010, conceding how many points? a) 240 b) 250 c) 260

Quiz 20: Answers

1. Vince Lombardi 2. Atlanta 3. Winning 4. Mike Sherman and Mike McCarthy 5. Wayne Larrivee 6. Larry McCarren 7. True 8. Houston Texans 9. James Lofton 10. Jerry Kramer 11. Detroit 12. True 13. Tom Coughlin 14. Cordarelle Patterson 15. Arrowhead 16. Lindy Infante 17. Tony Mandarich 18. Nick Barnett 19. b) 85F 20. a) 14

Quiz 22: 2010s

1. The Packers went 15-1 in the 2011 regular season, suffering their only loss to which AFC team?

2. The 2011 Packers were one and done in the playoffs, losing 37-20 to which team?

3. Which Green Bay back rushed for over 1,000 yards in both 2013 and 2014?

4. The 2012 and 2013 Packers were eliminated from the playoffs by which team?

5. Who was the offensive coordinator on the 2010 World Championship team?

6. Who was the defensive coordinator on that team?

7. The Packers tight ends coach in 2010 later became the head coach of an NFC East team. Can you name him?

8. The Packers had their first tie in over 25 years in November 2013, drawing 26-26 with which team?

9. The 2015 Packers suffered a heart-breaking 28-22 overtime loss to which team in the NFC Championship game?

10. The Packers lost in the playoffs in overtime a year later, losing 26-20 to which team?

11. In 2015, two players whose first name and surname start with the same letter led the team in touchdowns scored. Name the alliterative duo.

12. The Packers used back-to-back first round Draft picks in 2010 and 2011 to select which pair of offensive tackles?

13. Which USC Trojan linebacker did the Packers select with their first-round pick in 2012?

14. The Packers picked defensive backs in round one of the 2014 and 2015 NFL Drafts. Can you name the pair of players selected?

15. Which long-time Indianapolis Colt was voted to the Pro Bowl for the sixth time in his one and only season with the Packers in 2012?

16. Mason Crosby kicked a 51-yard field goal as time expired to give the 2016 Packers a 34-31 Divisional round win over which team?

17. The 2017 Packers endured their worst season in a decade, winning how many games?

18. The Packers acquired the services of quarterback DeShone Kizer following a trade with which team?

19. In which round of the 2013 NFL Draft did the Packers select running back Eddie Lacy? a) First b) Second c) Seventh

20. In the early part of the decade the Packers won how many straight NFC North titles? a) Three b) Four c) Five

Quiz 21: Answers

1. Pittsburgh 2. Packers 31-25 Steelers 3. Cowboys Stadium 4. Aaron Rodgers 5. Jordy Nelson 6. Greg Jennings 7. Nick Collins 8. Donald Driver, James Jones, Bryan Bulaga and Chad Clifton 9. Sixth seed 10. Matt Flynn 11. Philadelphia 12. Atlanta 13. Chicago 14. Clay Matthews 15. 10 wins 16. Deion Sanders 17. Christina Aguilera 18. The Black Eyed Peas 19. Brandon Jackson 20. a) 240

Quiz 23: Pot Luck

1. Who was the last Packers first-round draft pick whose first name and surname started with the same letter?

2. What does the B in the name of former defensive tackle B.J. Raji stand for?

3. Which long-time rival did the Packers defeat in the first ever game hosted at Lambeau Field?

4. In 1983, the Packers set an NFL record after scoring 49 points in the first half of a game against which team?

5. The Packers started the 2011 season by winning how many consecutive games?

6. Who are the two Packers to have made nine Pro Bowl appearances while with the team?

7. In what decade did the Packers wear green jerseys for the first time?

8. Who holds the team record for the most combined rushing and receiving yards in a single season with 2,250?

9. True or false – Six members of the Packers team made a cameo appearance as an a cappella group in the musical comedy, 'Pitch Perfect 2'?

10. Who are the two Packers to have amassed over 10,000 yards rushing and receiving?

11. Which Hall of Fame half back from the 1940s and 50s has had his number 3 jersey retired by the Packers?

12. What number jersey is worn by Pro Bowl offensive lineman David Bakhtiari?

13. Whose 322 catches for 4,223 yards are the most by a tight end in Packers history?

14. Which Dallas receiver's 'catch' was controversially ruled incomplete in the Cowboys' 2014 playoff loss to the Packers?

15. At which college are the Packers based during training camp?

16. True or false – Aaron Rodgers is the grandson of the composer Richard Rodgers?

17. The Packers played home games for 42 seasons at which Milwaukee stadium?

18. Immediately before becoming the head coach of the Packers Mike McCarthy had been the offensive coordinator of which team?

19. Complete the famous phrase associated with the Packers radio broadcasts – 'And there is your...'? a) dagger b) pistol c) rifle

20. How many regular season games did Brett Favre play for the Packers? a) 244 b) 255 c) 266

Quiz 22: Answers

1. Kansas City 2. New York Giants 3. Eddie Lacy 4. San Francisco 5. Joe Philbin 6. Dom Capers 7. Ben McAdoo 8. Minnesota 9. Seattle 10. Arizona 11. James Jones and Richard Rodgers 12. Bryan Bulaga and Derek Sherrod 13. Nick Perry 14. Ha Ha Clinton-Dix and Damarious Randall 15. Jeff Saturday 16. Dallas 17. Seven games 18. Cleveland 19. b) Second 20. b) Four

Quiz 24: Numbers Game

Identify the jersey number worn by the following Packers players.

1. James Lofton and Donald Driver

2. Charles Woodson and Ha Ha Clinton-Dix

3. LeRoy Butler and Nick Collins

4. Ryan Grant and Dorsey Levens

5. Bubba Franks and Jermichael Finley

6. Ryan Longwell and Tim Masthay

7. Chester Marcol and Chris Jacke

8. Clay Matthews and Frank Winters

9. Nick Barnett and Julius Peppers

10. Forrest Gregg and Bryan Bulaga

11. Robert Brooks and Jordy Nelson

12. Al Del Greco and Matt Flynn

13. Ed West and Antonio Freeman

14. Greg Jennings and Phillip Epps

15. Darren Sharper and Morgan Burnett

16. Quinten Rollins and Willie Wood

17. Josh Sitton and Santana Dotson

18. Sterling Sharpe and Javon Walker

19. Mark Murphy and Sam Shields

20. William Henderson and Micah Hyde

Quiz 23: Answers

1. Bryan Bulaga 2. Busari 3. Chicago 4. Tampa Bay 5. 13 games 6. Brett Favre and Forrest Gregg 7. 1930s 8. Ahman Green 9. True 10. Ahman Green and Donald Driver 11. Tony Canadeo 12. #69 13. Paul Coffman 14. Dez Bryant 15. St. Norbert College 16. False 17. County Stadium 18. San Francisco 19. a) Dagger 20. b) 255

Quiz 25: Anagrams

Rearrange the letters to make the name of a current or former Packers player or coach.

1. Arrange Doors

2. Fatter Verb

3. Combined Rival

4. Egg White Ire

5. Leather Springs

6. Mossy Carbon

7. My Metric Hack

8. Hen Manager

9. Jam Nets Fool

10. Robots Broker

11. Mends Hardwood

12. Animate For Neon

13. Joint Hosts

14. Only Deserves

15. Belly Router

16. Not Hounds

17. Shiny Racket

18. Amethyst Claw

19. Dab Cornball

20. Saved At Adman

Quiz 23: Answers

1. #80 2. #21 3. #36 4. #25 5. #88 6. #8 7. #13 8. #52 9. #56 10. #75 11. #87 12. #10 13. #86 14. #85 15. #42 16. 17. #71 18. #84 19. #37 20. #33

Made in the USA
Middletown, DE
17 February 2020

84912406R00033